fɪɴᴅɪɴɢ ʏᴏᴜʀ ᴍɪʟʟɪᴏɴ ᴅᴏʟʟᴀʀ
mate

RANDY POPE

finding your milLion doLLar

mate

NORTHFIELD PUBLISHING
CHICAGO

Scripture quotations, unless otherwise indicated, are taken from the New American
Standard Bible,® Copyright © The Lockman Foundation 1960, 1962, 1963, 1968, 1971,
1972, 1973, 1975, 1977, 1995. Used by permission.

All Scripture quotations marked NIV are taken from the Holy Bible, New International
Version.® NIV.® Copyright © 1973, 1978, 1984 by International Bible Society.
Used by permission of Zondervan Publishing House. All rights reserved.

Library of Congress Cataloging-in-Publication Data

Pope, Randy.
 Finding your million dollar mate / by Randy Pope.
   p. cm.
 ISBN 1-881273-76-8
 1. Mate selection. 2. Mate selection--Religious
aspects--Christianity. I. Title.
 HQ801.P75 2004
 646.7'7--dc22

                         2003020733

                 3 5 7 9 10 8 6 4 2

        Printed in the United States of America

To my wife, Carol, who for nearly three decades
has modeled the true meaning of a million dollar mate.
Thank you for such a blessed marriage.

Something You Should Read

This book is not simply about finding a spouse, but finding the right spouse. In fact, it's even more. It's about finding the right spouse for you for the long haul—a spouse you can love more at the end of a lifetime together than at its infatuated beginning.

I predict it will take the average reader between one and two hours to read this brief book. I also predict that the principles learned during this time will save many of its readers thousands of dollars spent on counseling, hundreds of hours of sleepless nights, and, more importantly, untold amounts of heartache experienced by oneself, one's spouse, one's children, one's parents, and countless numbers of others caught in the throes of a painful marriage and perhaps divorce.

As I write this book, I pray that you and countless others will experience the wonder of a great marriage. I'm convinced that hope for such a marriage begins in finding what I call "Your Million Dollar Mate."

contents

"Enjoy life with the woman whom you love all the days of your fleeting life . . . for this is your reward."

so you want to get married?

What if you could find the perfect mate, someone you could live with the rest of your life, who would meet all your longings and expectations? What would that kind of match be worth to you? I think you'll agree it would be priceless! That's exactly what this book is about . . . finding *your* million dollar mate.

Marriage is a big deal to anyone looking for that special someone with whom to spend the rest of his or her life. Everywhere I go it's on people's minds.

During a recent visit to Chicago I struck up a chat with a taxicab driver. I said, "Where are you from?"

"Pakistan," he answered.

Fascinated, I ventured a few questions to get him to open up. "How can you stand this weather in Chicago?" I asked casually.

"I hate it. I absolutely hate it," he retorted. "I've been here fourteen years, but I'm moving to California to get away from it." At that point he grew animated and said, "But first I'm going back to Pakistan to get married." After congratulating him, I asked him to tell me about his bride-to-be. He replied, "I don't know her. We've never met. Our marriage has been arranged."

My interest level intensified as I urged him to explain. He gladly continued, his eyes darting in and out of view in the rearview mirror as he navigated the congested Chicago streets. "No, I've never met her," he said, grinning. "I'll go home and give her an engagement ring, but we're not going to rush into it. After we get engaged we'll spend time getting to know each other."

"When you say you're not going to rush into it, how long will you actually be together before you get married?"

"Well, we're going to give it at least two months. That should be plenty of time."

Wow! An arranged marriage and only two months of dating! That's how they do it in Pakistan.

Obviously the methods for finding a mate are as numerous as there are cultures and lands.

And options abound for anyone who chooses to begin the mate quest. People can search on-line, go to a matchmaking party, or try their hand with a tarot-card reader. I recently read about dating nightclubs designed to allow singles to meet several eligible people in one night. When the bell rings each person moves around the room and strikes up a conversation with someone of interest. Conversations are timed. After twelve minutes another bell sounds and each person shuffles to the next person. Each time the people are hoping to learn as much as they can about whatever person they happen to be talking to. And in twelve minutes the expectation is that they will be able to size that person up, get a read on the chemistry between the two of them, and by the end of the evening, narrow the choice. The results are tabulated and matches are made. Imagine that. I call it icebreaker dating!

Even reality TV has cashed in on the business. Since so many people dream about finding that special someone, reality dating shows have struck instant gold.

The world has grown obsessed with reality dating. First on the scene was *The Bachelor*, then *The Bachelorette*. Following that, *Joe Millionaire*. And soon after, *Married by America* and *For Love or Money*, and, of course, *Cupid*. By the time this book is printed, there'll be many more. The wildest of all is *Mr. Personality*! Producers drape masks over the faces of a group of guys, half of them decent looking, the other less than handsome, parade them in front of an eligible woman, and say, "OK, you pick, but you'll never know what they look like until you've made your decision." Now that's what I call a blind date!

unreal expectations of a reality culture

Sadly, there's nothing *real* about reality TV. Especially in the dating craze. A journalist writing for the *Christian Science Monitor* interviewed a group of singles as they watched back-to-back episodes of these wild dating games. The article chronicles their reactions and reveals the unreality of reality TV:

While the unscripted TV craze now includes everything from celebrity "moles" in Hawaii to Allen Funt [Candid Camera] versions of high school reunions, dating remains a popular topic for the genre. This week two new shows debuted to predictably high ratings for a culture always fascinated by the spousal quest. . . . "How can you say these shows are about relationships?" asks 15-year-old Whitney Williams, sitting cross-legged on the rug and leaning forward attentively. "All they're doing is lying to each other. Relationships are supposed to be based on trust."

The idea of finding the perfect mate on television is met with a snort of derision from 23-year-old Melissa de la Rama. But then, she adds, maybe they're just looking for love. "I guess I don't blame them for looking for love in a weird place."[1]

I'm with her. I don't blame these young people for looking for love. We all desire that, don't we? Yet the results are coming in on the staying power of these matches made in TV land, and the news looks grim. Total devastation. Reality dating wreaks havoc, especially in the lives of those not chosen. Under the lights and cameras of that world of make believe, excited contestants make it so far only to be eliminated. The consolation prize? More pain, hurt, and rejection while the world watches from its living room. You can get *that* anywhere.

Most leave having never even gotten to the proposal.
They simply weren't chosen by someone they'd just met.
Losers end up feeling, well, like *losers!*
Distraught over a breakup before a
get-together ever took place. The
expectations left the planet and went
into orbit.

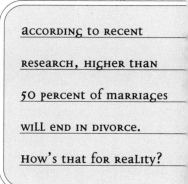

according to recent
research, higher than
50 percent of marriages
will end in divorce.
How's that for reality?

But are these "reality" shows really
so far removed from real life? Rates
for divorce and desertion climb
painfully higher each year. The statistics startle even the
most progressive soul. According to recent research, higher
than 50 percent of marriages will end in divorce. How's that
for *reality?*

Yet, despite such ominous projections, millions of
people continue to search for that perfect someone to grow
old with. In fact, if you're single and looking for a mate,
either for the first time or once again, you are among

approximately eighty million eligible singles in the U.S. alone! A recent census showed that out of all the householders accounted for in America, nearly half are unmarried adults. Many have never been married–about fifteen million people between the ages of twenty-five and thirty-four–and over twenty million of the single adults in the U.S. are single again following a divorce.[2] No wonder reality dating shows hit prime time with a bang!

18

is there really a perfect mate for me?

With so many options for finding that perfect someone and no shortage of eligible singles, why are the odds stacked so high against marriage? *I'm convinced there's something fundamentally wrong with the search process.*

Finding the right mate is a wonderful goal and a powerful desire in just about every person's life. Different cultures approach it in different ways. But whether it's Pakistan or Paducah, finding the right mate is serious business.

If you have any interest in marriage, the big questions
you're likely asking are, *Who will it be? How will I find that
person? And how do I know when I do?* Perhaps the most
important question of all: *How do I keep from becoming
another bleak statistic?*

I believe there *is* a way to find lasting fulfillment in
marriage—to find that match truly made in heaven. But
you likely won't find him or her on a game show or in
some trendy, smoke-filled piano bar or even on the Internet.
Finding the mate who's best for you is about deciding
what matters most. That requires honest reflection about
what drives you in life and determining your overarching
purpose for living.

LookiNG Back

The mere fact you've picked up this book and started reading tells me you're wondering about marriage . . . or you care deeply about someone else who is wondering about getting married.

Quite likely, you're single, have done some dating either in high school or in college or both, and now you're standing in the real world wondering if Mr. Right or Ms. Right truly exists. It may be that you're single again after a divorce or following the death of your spouse–in either case you're no doubt still wrestling with many tender and often conflicting emotions vying for control.

Whatever your situation I want you to know you're OK. No matter where you are in your process, what you're feeling as you read is perfectly normal. Being single does not make you a stranger in the land.

In fact, now would be an appropriate place for me to make some clarifying comments about being single.

I don't want you to believe that since I'm writing a book about finding your million dollar mate that marriage is for everybody. I don't believe that at all. But I am convinced that both being single and being married are gifts from God. If you subscribe to the notion, as I do, that there exists for you a divine design, then that design includes either the gift of marriage or the gift of singleness. Each gift comes with its own set of wonderful blessings and challenges. And if God's plan for you is to be single then He promises to provide you with everything you need to accept and even embrace that plan as part of His calling on your life.

Everything about the culture in which you and I live contradicts that perspective. And that's precisely why I felt compelled to write this book. But as we will soon see, culture is not a reliable guide as to what is best for you or for your life.

What I want to do in the pages that follow is help

guide you through the maze—to navigate the tossing sea of questions and emotions and help you land safely on the other side.

I've been there . . . right where you are. And in my nearly three decades of working and counseling with couples, I've journeyed nearly every path with people like you. So let's explore together and see what we discover!

But before we go there, take some time to reflect on what you've read. A section that I will call "Think About It" will end each chapter. This brief section will help you reflect on what you've read and prepare you to go on to the next chapter.

THINK ABOUT IT

How are you feeling? Choose the emotion that best fits:

Skeptical   **Curious**

Anxious   **Can't wait to turn the page!**

What are the reasons you decided to read this book?

How often do you think about marriage these days? Do you think there really is someone just right for you with whom you could spend the rest of your life? Why or why not?

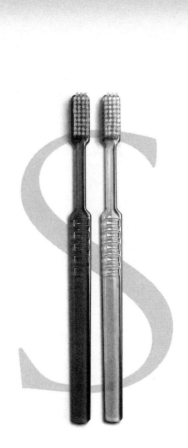

"Riches and honor are with me,
enduring wealth and righteousness.
My fruit is better than gold ... and
my yield better than choicest silver."

my MILLION DOLLAR
mate

As a college student I had to make three major decisions in life, decisions that stood above all others: *Who would be my master? What would be my mission?* and *Who would be my mate?* I came to the decision of Master while in high school, but it wasn't until my years studying at the University of Alabama that my decision about my Master began to radically impact my major life decisions.

Actually each of us has only one master–that one driving force behind all that we do. It becomes the compelling drive of our lives. For some the master is self—an obsession with satisfying those inner wants and passions. When self reigns, everything the person does feeds an insatiable appetite for self-satisfaction and fulfillment. Others have confessed being mastered by a deep longing to achieve significance—to leave a legacy, something by which they can be remembered when they're gone from this earth. That longing for significance drives them to achieve more and more. Many more are under the rule of money. Financial gain controls them. Money becomes their master. They work harder and harder to stockpile more and more.

At one time or another I have served nearly all of them. I have experienced a divided allegiance from time to time as well. You probably have too.

You see, each of us freely decides who or what will be our master. That's a willful, conscious, intellectual decision. I confess I was speeding toward the goal of self-fulfillment when I came to a fork in the road. It was then I learned that God loved me so much that He sent His Son to die on the cross and provide me with an eternal hope. God in His kindness delivered me from a path of destruction and set me free from a life lived for self. His was a free gift He offered through Jesus. He did everything; I surrendered through faith. Plain and simple. God became my *Master*.

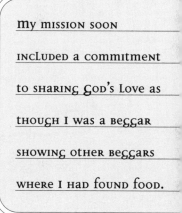

my mISSIOn SOON INcLUDED a commItment to SHaRINC CoD's Love as tHoUCH I was a BeCCaR SHowINC otHeR BeCCaRs wHeRe I HAD foUnD fooD.

From that decision would flow my *mission*, a lifelong vocation. My life had been significantly affected by individuals who had committed their lives to serving God vocationally, and I had come to understand the power of a life lived focused on helping others on their spiritual journey. My mission soon included a commitment to sharing God's love as though I was a beggar showing other beggars where I had found food. The decision of Master and mission would determine my future direction of life—ultimately shaping my third major life decision.

That final decision now could be made—who would be my *mate*? Where did getting married fit into the larger picture? Was marriage in the plan for me? If so, how would I know when I found the right woman? How could I be convinced the marriage would last? Those were major issues for me.

When all is said and done, an appropriate choice of mate would boil down to the answer to three questions: Does she love my Master? Does she embrace my mission? Does she have the qualities necessary to be my mate? And, of course, can she answer the same three questions regarding me?

wHat wiLL i caLL HeR?

Not long after I had settled the issues of my Master and mission, I started praying for my future mate. I assumed

I had not yet met her. Still, I felt compelled to bring her before the Lord each night in prayer. That prayer time became a tender routine. Before bed I would pray, "Lord, I don't know who she is. I don't know where she is or whether I've even met her. But I ask You to bless her and to protect her. I ask You to take care of her, provide for her, and keep her pure. Thank You, Lord. Amen."

That was it. That was my prayer. And I prayed it consistently night after night.

One day I thought, *I need a name for her. What am I going to call her?* It became important to me to identify this unknown person as I prayed. I knew I'd rather have a good spouse than a million dollars. Finding God's best for me would be worth more to me than any amount of money. So I started calling this mystery girl my *million dollar mate.* With that I revised my prayer to simply say, "God, please bless my million dollar mate."

a name that stuck

Funny how things like that catch on quickly. Many of my buddies began to hear me referring to my million dollar mate. The phrase became a household word. Eventually, I started hearing them talking about their "million dollar mates" too. That whole idea of finding someone worth more than any amount of money instantly struck a chord with my closest friends. They knew what I meant. They understood why I prayed night after night for that special girl. We all desired the very best we could find. And I'm sure you do too.

> that whole idea of finding someone worth more than any amount of money struck an instant chord with my closest friends.

My expectations soared as I prayed and dreamed about finding my million dollar mate. Life could not have been better.

Unfortunately, life has a way of knocking us flat when we think we've got things under control. That's exactly what happened to me. What took place next hit me broadside. It all started on a summer afternoon with a note from my dad and a painful jolt back to reality.

ReaLIty CHeCK

While I was out of town, my dad wrote a note and left it for me to read. The note read: "Good-bye. I will never see you again. If you ever marry and have children please kiss my grandchildren for me. I know you will never understand but good-bye forever." That was it. The shock of it all left me numb and stunned.

At first, I could only hope it was a joke. Yet we weren't laughing. My mother was numb with shock, fear, anguish; you name it. He was gone. His personal belongings, gone. It was done. Dad had left without a trace or an explanation. None of it made sense to me.

My father and I had always been close. We enjoyed much in common and maintained an unusually strong,

emotionally stable relationship. We didn't argue or fight—
in fact, we displayed much affection toward one another.
To me he epitomized true strength and character. He was a
role model to me and to almost everyone who knew him.

Many in our city held him in high regard, both as a
civic and a religious leader. He had established a thriving
dental practice and built our family a spacious, beautiful
home. Really, he had it all. Still the unimaginable happened.

Months went by as we searched in vain for my father.
We had no idea where to look. He left no clues. The trail
went cold. Then a strange course of events put us onto a
path that led us to him. Though he resisted my initial
requests for a visit, I eventually prevailed and set up a time
to meet. Nothing in the world could have prepared me for
what I'd learn about my dad, his broken marriage, and the
cold realities of life.

HaUNtiNG WORDS

When that day finally came, I invaded his strange new world, sat down across from him, and asked him squarely, "Why? You gave up everything. Why did you do it?"

You know why he did it? Simply put, he was unhappy in his marriage. Nearly emotionless, he said, "Son, you can't understand this now. Obviously I've been married longer than you have been alive. You've got to know that I loved your mother very, very much when I married her. We had many wonderful years together. Don't get me wrong." And then he spoke the haunting words that would make me start doubting my own hope for a permanent, happy marriage. He said, "Son, things change with time, and you're going to learn that one day. Things just change."

That was it. Things just change. That was his explanation. After twenty-five years of marriage, he cashed it all in because, in his words, *things just changed.* Needless to say I was stunned. We had what I thought to be a near-perfect family. Two cars. A beautiful home in a fabulous neighborhood. We took fun family vacations, attended church on Sunday, and lived as upstanding citizens. What could he mean *things change?* There had to be more to it than that!

I left confused . . . disillusioned . . . angry. *How could it be that simple? How could leaving a relationship be that easy?* A flood of questions and emotions raged in my mind, until finally the truth crashed ashore like a tidal wave. Dad was right.

During that time I'd been dating a girl I cared for deeply. But I had to admit I had dated other girls for whom I had experienced similar feelings. Moreover, throughout high school I had gone through a string of dating relationships where at the beginning of each one I thought I had found what I really wanted. But within a matter of months the relationship had ended. And what was frightening was that in each case the relationship seemed to break apart because "things changed." What began as a rush of sky-high emotions eventually vanished like vapor. Since nothing bound me to any given girl, I'd simply pick up and move on. It truly was that simple.

I had fallen into the same cycle, just like my dad. I knew I cared much for the girl I was dating at the time. In fact, she would eventually become my wife. Still, all things considered, I'd have bet money things would change with her too, and my desire to be with her would end. Just like all the rest. Just like my dad's marriage, and even more frightening, just like *his* dad's marriage–as I was later to learn.

I determined then to break that cycle. I simply could not let what happened to my folks happen to me.

> WHat BeGaN as a RUSH of sky-HIGH emotIoNs eventuaLLy vaNISHeD Like vapoR. SINce NothING BOUND me to any GIVeN GIRL, I'D sImpLy pIck up aND move oN.

Somehow I'd figure a way to avoid making such a huge mistake. My resolve was certain. There had to be a way to guarantee my marriage would go the distance. But how could I change this? Would my treasured routine of praying for my million dollar mate be enough to guarantee I'd not make the wrong decision? Those questions and sheer determination set me on a quest. I began a journey to discover the secret to finding my million dollar mate. What I had experienced with my parents' breakup drove me to find the answer.

Looking Back

Two-thirds of the marriages that end in divorce do so because of what people commonly refer to as *irreconcilable differences*. These are code words for "things change." Somehow, once the glow and glamour of a passionate romance dim, there's little left to keep a relationship vibrant. After the honeymoon fades into history, the hard work of compromise, righting wrongs, honest communication, and reconciliation begins. That's the stuff of lifelong marriages.

Often relationships begin ablaze with passion and romance, only to quickly cool under the duress of life's blustery assaults. Without a clear understanding of the big picture and a lifelong commitment to the relationship, the fire begins to wane, dwindles to a flicker, and eventually goes out. Or as my dad would describe it, "things change." That sounds oversimplified. But after nearly thirty years of working closely with couples struggling to remain married, I can say that's pretty much the score. Pretty grim, huh? Well, the news gets better as you read on. Trust me. Still, we're better off facing the tough realities up front. Before you go any further, spend a few minutes reflecting on what you've read in this chapter.

think about it

How did hearing my parents' story make you feel?

Can you describe a similar situation in your life or in the life of a friend or relative?

What emotions do thoughts of marriage conjure up for you?

"The way of a fool seems right to him,
but a wise man listens to advice."

two pictures worth a thousand words

What began as a casual interest in marriage became a passionate pursuit of truth. My resolve led me to develop a strategy of discovery. I interviewed a number of married people whom I respected and who had experienced fulfilling, lifelong marriages. What I was seeking was a common thread—a determining characteristic present in each of the successful relationships. I wanted to see something that made the difference. If I could find that, I knew I could crack the code.

And crack it I did. Each time the same principles emerged. As I interviewed these remarkable individuals I found the same ingredients for success. Don't get me wrong. None of these people I interviewed pretended to have perfect marriages. All of them confessed hardship along the way. They had known good times *and* bad times. Some confessed that some days their marriages hung together by a thread. But what a powerful thread that turned out to be!

I took the data I had gathered and condensed it into two simple diagrams that illustrate what I learned. I can't even begin to describe the response I've had as I've shared these two pictures with single people, young and old and everywhere in between. On nearly every occasion they've responded with statements like "That is so important! That's helpful to me!" Let me give you a couple of examples.

a tough sell

Fresh out of college and still single, I accepted a position as a pastor to singles in an old established church. While there I got to know a surgeon who asked me if I'd be willing to try to reach his college-age son. He expressed concern for the young man's direction in life and thought he would benefit from our relationship. I agreed to give it a shot.

One day I drove to the surgeon's home and spotted the father and son in the driveway washing a beautiful boat. As I pulled up the drive the son saw me coming and started toward the house.

Earlier I had asked his father if there were any common interests that we perhaps might share. His dad knew that I worked out on a regular basis, so he said, "My son is an attractive guy, but he's not in very good physical condition, and it bothers him. He keeps talking about working out but never does. Perhaps you could give him a few pointers." I figured that was a start.

As the young man headed for the house, his dad urged him to return and meet me. Grudgingly, he turned and made his way back to the driveway. We shook hands politely, and I said, "Your dad tells me you're interested in working out." Embarrassed, he answered, "Well, I'm interested in trying to get started." That was all I needed to hear. I suggested a time when we could meet, and he reluctantly agreed.

On the first day that we met at the health club he gave all the signals telling me to back off on the spiritual stuff. The walls were up! Sensitive to his reluctance I said, "Are you concerned that I'm going to be talking to you about God?"

"Absolutely," he answered, somewhat surprised by my directness. So I made a deal with him. I told him I wouldn't talk about spiritual matters unless he brought up the topic first. That, of course, seemed fine with him. And so we started our workout.

It wasn't long before he looked me straight in the eye

and said, "Can I ask you a question? I realize you're single and a preacher-to-be, but tell me, you have sex, don't you?" I tried not to show how startled I was by his question, and I explained that I had not had sex and I was committed to waiting until I married. "Come on! You're lying to me," he insisted. He didn't believe me for a minute! We agreed to drop the subject for the time being, and we left the weight room to begin swimming laps.

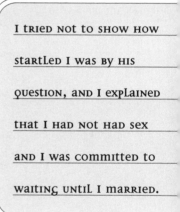

I TRIED NOT TO SHOW HOW STARTLED I WAS BY HIS QUESTION, AND I EXPLAINED THAT I HAD NOT HAD SEX AND I WAS COMMITTED TO WAITING UNTIL I MARRIED.

As I neared the end of the pool after a few laps, he came swimming up behind me out of breath and asked once again, "You do, don't you?"

I said, "I do what?"

He said, "You do have sex. Come on, be honest. Preachers don't lie, do they?"

I said, "I don't have sex. I never plan to until the day I

get married." He remained unconvinced.

We then headed to the sauna. We sat sweating, wrapped in towels, waiting to hit our time limit when he piped up again saying, "Come on. Please tell me. You do, don't you?"

I said, "Are you still talking about sex?"

He said, "Yeah, you do, don't you?"

I said, "No, I don't. Do you want to know why I don't have sex?"

He said, "Yes, I do!"

My opportunity had arrived. I found a piece of paper and a pen and drew two diagrams—which illustrate the all-important principles I learned from my numerous interviews. He stared at the diagrams bewildered and expressionless. As I drew them I explained what they meant. Lights blinked on in his head. I said calmly, "This is the reason I don't have sex. I'm looking for something totally different."

I crumpled the paper to throw it away when he stopped

me and said, "Don't do that. I want that piece of paper!"

"Why?" I asked in surprise.

He said, "Well, I want to be able to show people what we believe."

I said, "We?! You got a mouse in your pocket?! What are you talking about, 'we'?" He went on to tell me that he valued my perspective regarding sex and marriage, even if that perspective included God. From that point on, he was more than willing to talk about spiritual things.

Not long after that I met an attractive girl who had grown up in a prominent family but who had just become engaged to a big-time drug pusher. The same thing happened. Her dad, concerned about his daughter's future, asked if I'd try to talk to her.

She showed up at a class for singles I had begun teaching at a friend's home. After one session I introduced myself and asked if she had a few minutes to talk. I told her I knew she had gotten engaged, and I asked if I could show her a couple of diagrams that might help prepare her for marriage. She agreed to talk, and I showed her the diagrams. I explained to her what the diagrams meant and how important it was that she thought hard and honestly about her decision to marry. Within a few days she had called off her engagement and eventually broke off the relationship.

On another occasion I had that same conversation and drew the same two diagrams for a young man involved in a serious dating relationship. He was headed full steam toward the altar. But the outlook for that marriage looked bleak too. After seeing the diagrams and listening to my explanation, he also ended his relationship with the woman he had been intending to marry. And the stories go on and on.

Hɪᴛᴛɪɴɢ a ɴᴇʀᴠᴇ

I've shared those same principles with countless young

people searching for that special someone. And in nearly every case the reaction is the same. Many thought they had found *the one*, only to discover they had nearly made the mistake of their lives. In many other cases, people have been reassured that they're on the right track.

One day I received an invitation to go to the University of Georgia to share the diagrams with one of the leading sororities on campus. I gladly accepted the invitation, not knowing what to expect. I figured a small number of girls would attend. To my surprise, the place was packed. I couldn't believe the interest in the subject. I talked for about forty minutes, shared the diagrams, and ended with prayer. I expected the place to empty like a fourth-grade class on the last day of school. Few people left. Slowly girls began to inch their way up to the front of the room to talk.

> Many thought they had found *the one*, only to discover they had nearly made the mistake of their lives.

There I stood in the middle of a major university, surrounded by girls I'd never met, talking to them about marriage. It was amazing.

Word spread quickly, and soon I received numerous invitations to speak to other groups on campus. The idea of finding a million dollar mate had struck a nerve.

So many people head in the wrong direction hoping to find that perfect someone, only to discover heartache and pain at the end of the road. That doesn't have to be your story. If you're willing to hang in there with me and open your mind to a different way of thinking about how to find a marriage partner, I don't think you will regret it.

In the next couple of chapters I want to share with you what I've shared with hundreds, maybe thousands, of people like you—a set of profound principles, illustrated by two simple diagrams, that just may benefit your life.

Looking back

I want you to start thinking in new ways about the process of finding a mate. Many people I've talked to about these principles thought they were doing *me* a favor by listening . . . at first. Maybe that's why you've picked up this book. Your mother or your father or a friend has urged you to read it. Whatever your reason, I'm convinced you'll find something of value here, if you're able to keep an open mind. Don't put the book down out of frustration or because you think this is another plot to persuade you to get more religious. There's so much more to what I want you to understand than that. Stay with it, OK? You may be in for a wonderful surprise.

think about it

Why do you think there is so much interest in the topic of dating and marriage in today's society?

How do television and Hollywood portray dating, relationships, and marriage?

In what ways has your own thinking been impacted by pop culture?

What are the top three things you're looking for in a serious relationship?

"Charm is deceitful and beauty is vain."

fataL
attractions

The quote on the opposite page is how one ancient poet summed up the virtues of outward appearances. He understood human nature like few people, and he knew that outward appearances mean too much. Little has changed in the thousands of years since those profound words were penned. Men and women today spend billions of dollars each year on designer clothing, brand-name makeup, face-lifts and cosmetic surgery, fitness trainers, perfumes and colognes—all with the goal of sprucing up the outside. Sadly, only scant attention is usually given to what I call cultivating the inner life. Outward expressions of beauty sell. Muscles sell. That's what attracts the opposite sex. The result is an entire culture built upon the superficial.

Let me make the first of two crucial statements at this point: *The typical couple builds their relationship upon what I call fatal attractions.* Two people are drawn together through a mysterious blend of alluring physical traits and engaging personality characteristics. But the physical appearance and the personality are not the full picture. Take a look at the first diagram on page 57. Diagram 1 illustrates what I mean.

Looks, charm, and so much more

A person is essentially made up of three facets—the body, the personality, and the spirit. The body quite obviously represents the outward appearance—a person's frame, hair color, body size, and so on. We humans come in all shapes

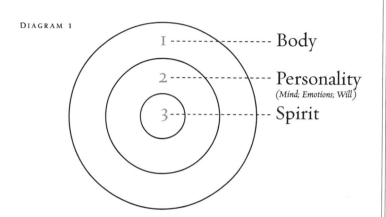

DIAGRAM 1

and sizes. Beyond that we work tirelessly at conveying to the world that we're models of confidence, charisma, and electrifying intellect. That's the *personality*. Personality comprises a person's wit, his or her mind, manners, behaviors, and much more. All these qualities are external expressions. What cannot be so easily identified is the stuff of the spirit–the third circle in the diagram–the deep, inner makeup of an individual. Look again at Diagram 1. The concept is both simple and profound. The three circles represent the multiple core aspects of your person. We all have a physical part of our being, and we also have a personality—the composite of our minds, our emotions, and our wills. We also have a part of our being called the spirit or the soul. Your body, personality, and spirit all come together to form *you*.

As I did my investigation, asking numbers of people about their lifelong marriages, I concluded that most relationships begin with an intense focus on the first two circles—the body and the personality—very much an outward attraction. Think about it: that's likely true about most relationships you and I have been in. A man is drawn by a woman's shapely figure. A woman finds herself more often attracted to guys with great personalities. Ladies like guys who listen, make them laugh, and have the rare ability to maintain engaging, sensitive conversations. That's personality plus!

Surprisingly, none of those things made the list that kept a marriage alive and healthy for the long haul. Marriages that never moved out of circles 1 and 2 strayed into "at-risk" territory after a decade or so. We will look at the reasons for that shortly. Marriages that went the distance . . . the relationships that had assurance of lasting over a long period of time . . . had at some point in the process shifted from focusing on physical and personality attractions to investing in what I call "spiritual attractions."

Certainly this is not to say that only marriages with such soul attractions can experience permanence and happiness. But it is to say that only relationships of this type can have the high probability of such long-term fulfillment.

SHOEBOXES AND LOVE LETTERS

Unfortunately, that didn't happen in my parents' marriage. But you wouldn't have known that from how their relationship began. About the time my folks were breaking up, I was, as I mentioned, dating my wife, Carol. But she was living in a different city, so we were corresponding by letter (those were pre-Internet days!). While desperately attempting to piece together some sense to the whole ordeal, I stumbled across a shoebox filled with notes and cards my mother had collected from years past. She cherished them enough to keep them for more than twenty-five years. They were primarily love letters between her and my dad from their early days of dating.

I compared my parents' Love Letters to my Letters to Carol and thought, *Man, this stuff makes my Letters sound Like interoffice memos!*

Slowly, one by one, I read each tender expression of love and devotion my mom and dad had written. I couldn't believe what I was reading. They were filled with words and phrases that made me chuckle, then anguish, then chuckle again. They were full of romantic expressions of love. Passion flowed from one letter to the next. As I read, I compared my parents' love letters to my letters to Carol and thought, *Man, this stuff makes my letters sound like interoffice memos!* Theirs had a depth of intensity I had rarely expressed.

To a certain degree I wasn't surprised. They did come from the same socioeconomic background. They enjoyed their parents' approval of marriage, and they were similar in age. They shared much in common, not the least of which was a deep commitment to religious things. Once they were married they committed to each other to pray together before going to bed. Sadly, my parents' religion was not the genuine item. They were not *real* Christians —even by their own admission many years later. But they talked the talk and kept all the right rules. That's why they determined to have the kind of marriage that valued time in prayer together as a couple. All in all, from the outside looking in, they had a great marriage. And it was pretty good for many years, but then it disintegrated before our eyes. All that was left was dust and rubble. Their relationship had never managed to move from a focus on the first two circles, the body and the personality.

Tragically, that's how most marriages begin, and why ultimately many end. But the more people I interviewed, the more convinced I became that what most people are looking for in a mate are physical attractiveness and personality plus. If you're fully honest with yourself, you'll admit you've been there too. Let me ask you a question. If you're a guy reading this book, what is the first thing that attracts you to a woman? You got it. The physical. You're looking at what she's got in the way of looks!

That's the physical aspect of a person—the outermost circle in Diagram 1! Guys are typically most concerned about what a woman looks like. It doesn't matter if she's beautiful to the world. But if she's beautiful to him the beholder, that's what counts.

If you're a woman reading this book, let me ask you the same question. What's the first thing you look for in an eligible man? Sure, I know you like a guy who is good-looking. But what's *most* important to you?

Personality! Right? Sure that's right. Women prefer men who are confident but gentle and considerate. Funny but appropriate and tasteful. Engaging but not stuck on themselves. Sensitive yet strong and protective. You know what that is? Personality! Circle 2.

Let me explain what I mean. Whenever I'm in an audience and I'm giving this message to a large group of young singles, I say to the skeptics, "I can prove that this is true." I invite them to look around the group of people listening to the message and notice how many beautiful girls are dating, let me say, "less-than-handsome" guys! Everyone laughs, realizing I'm kidding, but they rarely miss the obvious. There have been times when I've looked at an average-looking guy and seen the knockout girl at his side, and I'm tempted to say, "Wow! How did you get her?" I've never asked that, but I hope you understand my point. He's got a whole lot more going for him in the personality department than in the physical. Quite often it's the other way around for the women. Either way, the physical and personality traits are the major attractants. But there's the rub! Neither lasts long enough to sustain a lifelong marriage.

THINGS THAT DECREASE

As I thought more about my parents and the people I had interviewed, the truth struck me like lightning. Ninety-nine percent of doomed relationships begin and end focusing on things that are *decreasing*. The body and personality both naturally decrease over time. Everything to do with physical appearance and personality expression is in decline.

My son and I were recently talking before I left for work when he said, "You know, I'm not having the same vigor and enthusiasm that I have had for working out." And I said, "Hey, you think it's hard *now* to keep up your motivation. Wait until there's no goal to get any further.

I'm trying to hang on and preserve my losses."
Unfortunately, he too quickly agreed!

You see, everything outward is in decline. My wife
and I tell the same story. Only in
recent years have she and I begun to
give great attention to what we eat. As
the years go by, we both notice we're
not as we once were and that we must
work harder at maintaining healthy
bodies. Things do change physically for
all of us.

> my wit, my sense of
> memory, and anticipation
> are all suffering under
> the strain of age.

The same is true of personality. A favorite game I
used to play with my kids when they were little was
Concentration—a memory game requiring a quick and
agile mind. I used to think I was good at it. I love to win
—and unlike most good fathers, even against my own
children. When my firstborn whipped me mercilessly at
only six years old, I knew my mind was in decline. My

wit, my sense of memory, and anticipation are all suffering under the strain of age. That's all part of a personality in decline. I'm not the spry, outgoing jokester Carol was initially attracted to. She's seen my rough edges, and they've scratched her raw at times. She knows the real, more fragile, often self-absorbed, impatient me. The personality-plus guy she met in the student union went AWOL somewhere along the way. You know what I mean. Personality is *decreasing.* Just like the body.

That was true of my parents as well. As I reflected on my years growing up, I began to see things that I never noticed as a child. The declining degrees of affection and quality time my mother and father spent together evidenced a relationship in decline. They had grown further and further apart as the years went by. Those things that initially attracted them to each other began to disappear, and so did the foundation for their marriage.

Piece by piece I began to put the puzzle together. At

first I felt only despair and disillusion. But the more the puzzle came together, hope began to emerge.

LookInG BacK

We are all made up of three parts—the body, the personality, and the spirit. Each is represented by one of the concentric circles in Diagram 1. Most people come together based on an initial outward attraction—the guys typically focusing first on the physical and secondarily on the personality. The girls typically focus first on the personality and secondarily on the body. The problem is that both body and personality eventually decline. Once the attraction disappears, the relationship starts to crumble. We all have seen it too many times to count.

Who wouldn't agree that's how most relationships begin and end—with a focus on things that *decrease?*

think about it

What are you attracted to in someone of the opposite sex?

In what ways does culture reinforce and overemphasize things that decrease?

In what ways do you see the principle of declining attractions applying to your current relationship?

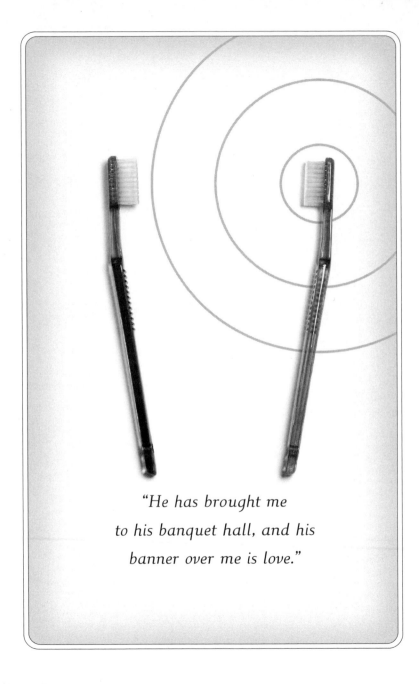

"He has brought me
to his banquet hall, and his
banner over me is love."

CHAPTER FIVE

THE gREatest
hope

I want you to look carefully now at Diagram 2 on page 73. I began to think of dating relationships this way. The typical dating cycle begins with two people who are attracted to each other. It starts casually and continues for a few weeks, maybe even for months, as the woman and man get to know each other. But over time, interest wanes, things begin to break down, and eventually the relationship ends. That's how it is with Jennifer, in Diagram 2. She's down at the bottom of the diagram. The men are those in her dating pathway. Here's how it often unfolds.

First, I hear that Jennifer has fallen for Trey. They date for a while, and they both think they've found love. I hear Jennifer talking about how in love she is with this guy. But it's not long before Jennifer loses interest in Trey and breaks up with him. Jennifer moves on to Josh. He's especially nice and a lot better communicator, and he enjoys doing more of the things Jennifer likes. Soon I hear Jennifer talk about how wonderful Josh is and that she's certain this is true love. Perhaps I say something like, "Jennifer, I thought you were in love with Trey. What happened?" She's quick to say things changed and it didn't work out. She didn't truly understand her feelings. I guess Trey was only a five-dollar guy!

The next thing you know, Jennifer loses interest in Josh also and breaks up with him, recognizing that he was only a ten-dollar potential mate.

Jennifer soon meets Bill, who appears to be her dream

DIAGRAM 2

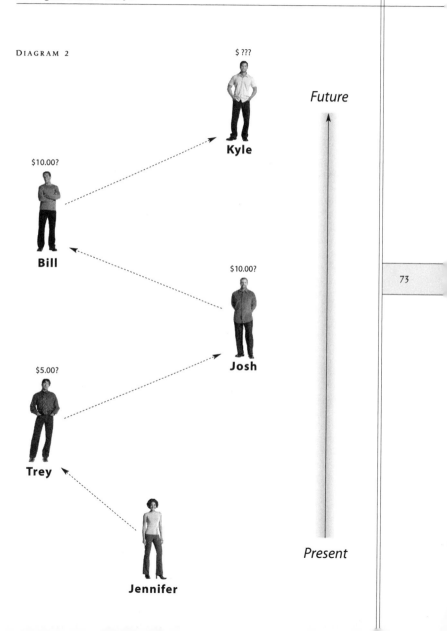

$???

Kyle

Future

$10.00?

Bill

$10.00?

Josh

$5.00?

Trey

Jennifer

Present

come true. I then hear Jennifer telling a friend how in love she is with Bill. Interrupting, I ask, "Jennifer, I thought you said you loved Josh."

"Oh," she responds, "how silly I've been. I only thought I knew what true love was. But now I know for sure." You guessed it. It's only months before feelings for Bill begin to fade. Before long, it's another breakup. The reason for the breakup was that Bill was only a ten-dollar Bill (pun intended!).

And now it's on to Kyle. Again it's love, love, love! But she would have to be asking herself, *How do I know this time that I've found what I'm looking for? Is it only because I've reached an age where marriage is expected?* How risky could a marriage be?

That's a pretty typical picture of the dating scene. I think you'd agree.

And even as you read you may be sensing you are trapped in that cycle. Many people are caught yet don't realize the problem. What we need is a fresh perspective.

JOINED at tHe SOUL

The first important statement I made was that the typical couple builds their relationship based on fatal attractions. Here's the second statement, equally important: *The greatest hope for a couple is to build a relationship upon a spiritual foundation.* That's a relationship that starts and continues with an emphasis on the innermost concentric circle, the spirit. (See Diagram 1 on page 57.) The body and personality aspects end up being fatal attractions—fatal to a lifelong marriage relationship. They simply don't provide the staying power for a fulfilling lifelong covenant of marriage. The only attraction that will last is a spiritual attraction—an attraction of the soul.

I once met a man who was many years my senior. He was a Golden Glove boxing champion who enjoyed life to the fullest. Despite his age, he looked like he was in remarkable physical condition. He had been invited to lead a seminar I attended in Southern California. During the course of the week he repeatedly referred to his "bride" with endearing words and love-filled expressions of adoration. Without a doubt, the man was crazy about this woman. And I'll be honest, judging by the way he went on and on about her, I thought perhaps he was one of those cradle robbers who had found himself a younger woman and was enjoying a youthful fling! Instead I learned a valuable lesson. He told us we'd finally get to meet his wife after she arrived a few days later. We were stunned by what we saw.

From the corner of the room came a frail, aged, but charming little old lady who met him on the platform. He tenderly helped her up. And with a huge grin, he said, "Folks, I'd like you to meet the love of my life!" There she stood. No knockout blonde with a thirty-something figure. No head-turning outfit that showed off a model-like frame. Though graceful and unassuming, she looked her age. I wondered how a man like him could get excited about a woman who could barely walk onto the platform. But now I know. She was his million dollar mate. They were joined at the soul.

I was so oriented to the fatal attraction that all I could think about was what she looked like. I could only assume she had decreased significantly in the realms of the body and personality. She looked old. She acted old. She was old. And then he said, "And you know what? I used to think that we were in love when we got mar-

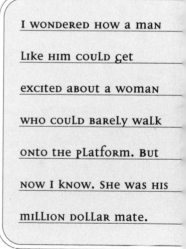

I WONDERED HOW a maN LIke HIM COULD get excited about a woman WHO COULD BaReLy waLk ONto the pLatform. But NOW I kNOW. SHe was HIS miLLION DOLLaR mate.

ried—and though we were, I do believe in the first five years of our marriage our love doubled. And in four years it doubled again, and now it's as if it doubles every day. I declare I love her more with each passing day." The place erupted in applause.

That's a marriage that will go the distance. My friend had found his million dollar mate. But why? What's the secret? That question kept me searching until I found the answer.

ᴛʜᴇ ᴜʟᴛɪmᴀᴛᴇ mᴀᴛᴇ

Let me explain what I mean. During my desperate search for perspective, following my parents' breakup, I discovered some words in the Bible that shed great light on my dilemma. In fact, the truths I found have revolutionized the way I think about dating.

The words were written two thousand years ago but remain as relevant today as they were when they were first penned.

Seeing that His divine power has granted to us everything pertaining to life and godliness, through the true knowledge of Him who called us by His own glory and excellence. For by these He has granted to us His precious and magnificent promises, so that by them you may become partakers of the divine nature, having escaped the corruption that is in the world by lust. Now for this very reason also, applying all diligence, in your faith *supply* moral excellence, *and in your* moral excellence, knowledge, *and in your knowledge,* self-control, *and in your self-control,* perseverance, *and in your* perseverance, godliness, *and in your godliness,* brotherly kindness, *and in your brotherly kindness,* love.[3]

Wow! How would you like to have a mate who possessed all those qualities? Faith. Moral excellence. Knowledge. Self-control. Perseverance. Godliness. Kindness. Love. Sounds like the ultimate mate. That's what happens when the divine nature is formed within a human soul. God sends His Spirit to dwell within our spirits, bringing about a supernatural salvation which produces such remarkable qualities (see Diagram 3 on page 81). Now that's worth waiting for, don't you agree? The qualities present in a million dollar mate are the result of a spiritual transformation.

The passage from the Bible you just read lists the qualities that truly matter—the ingredients of a lasting relationship. My boxing friend you just met had built on that foundation. Clearly, the physical and personality traits that first attracted this couple to each other decades earlier had almost vanished over time. But they hadn't lost what mattered most. And they were more in love in their eighties than they ever were in their twenties!

Yet none of that happened by accident. Something existed in their marriage that didn't exist in my parents' relationship. The more people I talked to and the more questions I asked, the more the truth came into focus. I finally began to understand some things that I had never understood in the past. Here's the truth: If you have number one—an attraction of the spirit—you don't mind so much when the body and the personality decline.

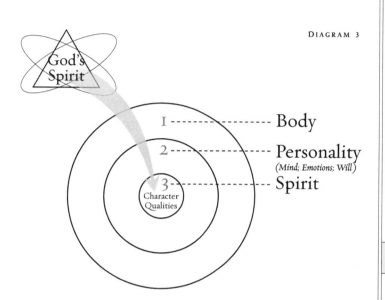

Diagram 3

wHat matteRs most

I served as a chaplain for about ten years on the pro-tennis circuit. It was not atypical after a particularly challenging singles match for the losing player to enter the locker room angry and frustrated. Perhaps he would curse and slam his fists into the lockers, then proceed to fling his racket across the floor. To this player, losing a singles match in a professional tournament meant total elimination. He had lost everything.

Often, though, in that same tournament, I might run into one of the players who had just lost a doubles match while still in contention in singles. Although he was a bit disappointed in the outcome, he knew he could still win the bigger prize. He could take losing the doubles match in stride because he hadn't lost what was most important. Do you get the idea? It's the same way in a marriage relationship. When you don't lose what's most important, losing lesser things doesn't matter.

What matters most in a relationship are the qualities needed for that relationship to last. And those qualities are not natural to any of us. They are the result of a *supernatural salvation*. Genuine spirituality is a supernatural act from start to finish.

That's what I call an emphasis on the soul. For the longest time, I thought that to be spiritual was all about

what I did *for* God. But that misses the mark. And though
that understanding prevails in our society today—that the
only path to God is to work hard enough or be good
enough to please Him—that perspective runs counter to
revealed truth. In your quest for a mate, don't look for
someone who's doing stuff for God. You need to find that
special someone who shows living evidence that God has
done something for him or her.

Looking Back

Everything we've talked about in this chapter happens as a result of *faith*. When you express true faith you become grounded in a relationship, not by works or by living a good life, but by faith in Jesus Christ and His death on the cross. And your faith, though primarily a foundation upon which to build a life of *moral excellence*, is a living faith that is reflected in the way you live. You can see it in how a person lives and relates to others and to God. In other words, the person chooses to live a life pleasing to God, not to earn His favor, but because he has experienced His favor. *Knowledge* simply means a relationship between the thing knowing and the thing being known. In knowing a human being, you have a relationship and you are getting to know better who the person is.

Self-control is the ability to stop when you want to keep going. *Perseverance* means you have the ability to keep on going when you'd rather stop. *Godliness* reflects a virtuous life, and *brotherly kindness* demonstrates you care deeply about the needs of others. There's a selfless quality to your living. The apex of it all is *unconditional love*–the ability to give without expecting anything in return. That's true love. A person with these kinds of traits is the kind of spouse you should be looking for.

Wouldn't you rather wait for that?

think about it

How are you feeling about what you've read so far?

To what degree do you value spiritual things? Have you ever thought about spiritual realities before now? Why do you think this is so important to the quest for finding your million dollar mate?

"I found him whom my soul loves."

aLL tHat
increases

As a little boy growing up, I heard that love makes the world go around. You've probably heard that too. Love is the number one emotion we pursue in all relationships. And the lack of it explains many of life's painful ills. But for years I also struggled with finding an adequate definition of love. Until I finally came to realize that true love originates in the divine and is a gift from the Creator God, I limped along in my inadequate view of it. Now, I think I've found one of the best definitions of love anyone can offer:

Love is a commitment based on the will of God, typically undergirded by an emotion.

For years I thought what my dad believed: Love was merely a feeling. I assumed that because that's what I had been taught. I recall as a kid asking my dad how I would know when I was in love. He said, "Son, you'll just know it. You'll feel it." Well, no wonder his marriage didn't last. When the emotion of love left, so did my dad.

But since God is love, true love comes from God and that love flows through our relationships.

Love in Real Life

Many years ago I met a man who for me epitomized success. I mean he had it all—looks, talent, brains—the works. Besides all that, he had five beautiful, blond-headed kids, each the model of good behavior. I was curious about what his wife looked like. If she matched every other aspect of this guy's life, she probably was some sort of cross between Cindy Crawford, Julia Roberts, and Sandra Bullock! When I finally met her I was shocked to see she wasn't all that I had expected. I eventually got close enough to this man to ask my question. I said, "Can you talk to me a little about love? What does love look like for you?"

He told me that for him love meant giving his wife the time she needed and making sure she felt his strong support. Love meant asking if there was anything he could do to lighten her load. Love meant spending time with their kids so his wife could have time to herself. He described love as a commitment that was undergirded by an emotion. He loved her by doing what he knew was best *for her*. He stayed more focused on the needs of his wife than on meeting his own needs. That's an ability that comes from above. It's a commitment, and it's based on what one knows to be the will of God.

tHINɢs that INCReasE

Let me take you back to the final verses in that passage from 2 Peter. Read carefully these final words:

*For if these qualities are yours and are **increasing**, they render you neither useless nor unfruitful in the true knowledge of our Lord Jesus Christ.*[4]

That's the secret. All these people I've mentioned who have experienced relationships that lasted focused on qualities that *increase*. They are spiritual qualities that continually increase in value and depth and that have little or nothing to do with outward appearances or personality traits. They represent the qualities that last.

When that finally sank in, I knew I couldn't go on as usual. At the time I was dating Carol, who would later become my wife. Though I could say without doubt that my strongest attraction to Carol was based on her spirit, I knew I had to find out if Carol's care for me was focused on those same qualities–qualities that increase rather than decrease over time. Only then would I know if she could be my million dollar mate.

On my next drive back to her hometown I prayed for wisdom. I would ask Carol a question, and her answer would tell me what I needed to know. I knew that Carol had strong feelings for me. But was it real love? I knew that if the wrong things were driving our relationship, then it would be fated for disaster.

> aLL tHeSe peopLe I've meNTIONeD WHO Have expeRIeNceD ReLaTIONSHIpS tHat LaSTeD focuSeD ON quaLITIeS tHat *INCRease*.

The moment came and we were alone. I took a deep breath and said, "Carol, I've got a question, and you have no idea the importance of your answer. You've got to be honest with me now more than ever. Why do you love me?" A bit surprised, she looked at me with her pretty brown eyes and said, "I'll tell you exactly why I want to be with you and why I think I love you. It's because of what's in your heart. I love you for what's inside of you." That's all I wanted to hear. I had found *my* million dollar mate!

My love for Carol has grown stronger throughout the years of our marriage. We've been married for twenty-eight years, and not once have I doubted God designed her to be with me. And I assure you, had it not been for our understanding of the nature of genuine love and the spiritual transformation I've just described, I'm not certain we'd be married today. I may have wound up being another statistic, just like my dad.

Lookinç back

Definitions of love abound in our society. Turn on the television in the evening and you'll find Hollywood's take on the matter. We've certainly demonstrated that none of those ideas have lasting merit. What we need is a divine perspective—a view of love from the Author of love.

You may be reading this and realizing you've never encountered a love like this. You're not convinced you've experienced a spiritual transformation by putting your faith in Jesus Christ. If not, then that is where you need to begin. There is nothing you or I can do to earn God's favor. Because of our desperate condition we need God to intervene. God draws us to Himself in love, and then we fall in love with Him. The deeper we grow in love with Him, the more we desire to give our lives to Him. Like in a loving marriage, the relationship grows deeper over time. God always initiates that loving relationship. All you need to do is respond to Him. You can do that by talking to

Him in prayer and asking Him to take control of your life. I've included some words that might help you talk with God, especially if you're doing so for the first time.

Dear God, thank You for showing interest in me by showing me Your love through Your Son Jesus Christ. I want to live my life for You and not for myself. I invite You to take control of my life—to bring about a spiritual transformation in me to help me be the kind of person You created me to be. I put my faith in You and in Your Son Jesus today. Thank You for loving me. Amen.

94

tHINk aBOUt It

Did you pray that simple prayer?

If so, I encourage you to find a Christian friend and tell that person about it. You've made a remarkable decision that will be verified over time by a changed life. You need to share your spiritual journey with someone who understands such a transformation.

For more information on what it means to be a Christian call 1-888-NEED HIM.

95

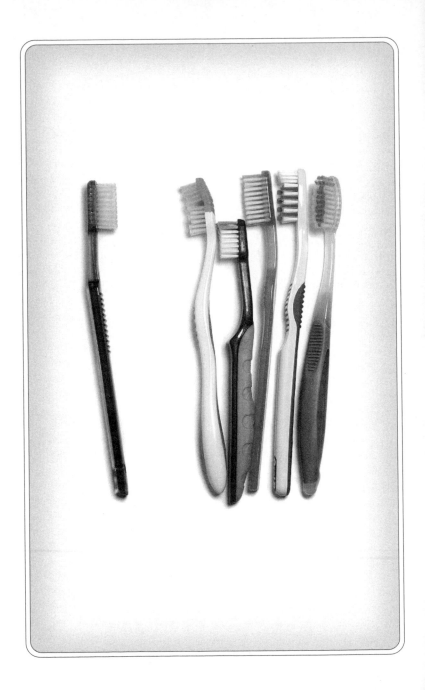

fiNDINÇ YOUR MILLION DOLLaR
mate

This chapter will describe five of the six principles I want you to put in place for finding your million dollar mate. Remember: Principles are not promises. They don't guarantee you'll find that special someone. God has a plan for you, and that may be to wait. Or He may desire that you remain single for an undetermined period of time or perhaps even for a lifetime. What I suggest here are only parameters that I believe will protect you and guard you from making decisions you'll later regret. If you're willing to trust God and trust His plan, you're already on the right path. Read each principle carefully and make certain you understand it before you move on to the next.

PRINCIPLE #1: DEVELOP A SPIRITUAL ATTRACTION IN YOUR LIFE.

In other words, ladies, if you want a king, you've got to be a queen. Guys, if you want a queen, you've got to be a king. By developing a life of faith, those royal qualities in the 2 Peter Zone—faith, moral excellence, knowledge, self-control, perseverance, godliness, brotherly kindness, and love—become the fabric of your life. These qualities represent the crucial building blocks for developing a spiritual attraction in your life.

PRINCIPLE #2: IF YOU'RE INVOLVED WITH SOMEBODY WHO IS NOT A POTENTIAL MILLION DOLLAR MATE, BREAK IT OFF IMMEDIATELY.

Make certain both you and the person you are dating

understand what matters most. You must both understand the importance of building on a foundation of faith. I've asked too many people if the person they are dating was a Christian, only to hear them say, "Weeeell . . . I *think* so." I tell them that's not good enough. There's too much at stake to leave that to doubt.

You ought to be able to say with certainty that the person you are considering as a lifelong mate has experienced a supernatural salvation—that God has begun a work in them through their faith in Jesus. If you don't believe that to be the case, then I suggest you're involved with the wrong person. You're building your relationship on the shaky ground of a fatal attraction.

When I met Carol she assumed she was a Christian but she really wasn't. She was moralistic, religious, and upstanding in the way she lived, but without having experienced a supernatural salvation. Eventually, she did become a Christian while in college and I began to see remarkable changes in her life. She showed evidence of having experienced a spiritual transformation. All those qualities we looked at in 2 Peter were being formed in her heart and reflected in her life. For instance, she would not have gone to inappropriate places physically, even if I had asked her to. She had *self-control*. She demonstrated courage to do things that she would never naturally do except for *perseverance*. And I realized she *was loving others and God unconditionally*. It was all there because she knew God, having become rightly related to Him. That's what you want to be able to say about the person you are considering marrying. You want the person to be living smack in the middle of the 2 Peter Zone and growing to greater degrees in those spiritual qualities! If you can't say that about the person, then call off the relationship—now.

PRINCIPLE #3: WHILE DATING, MAKE EDIFICATION YOUR ULTIMATE GOAL.

I'm not at all against dating. In fact, I'm convinced dating can be a positive aspect of an individual's development if gone about with the proper perspective. Do you want to know what dating is? Take some time to look at Diagram 4 on page 103. The word *dating* comes from a Latin word that means "to give," thus "to build up" or "to edify, to encourage." As a good friend of mine puts it, dating should be seen as a "**Divine Appointment To Edify.**" I'm all for edifying. If you find someone of the opposite sex that you'd like to edify, go for it! But that's a whole lot different from defrauding your partner by seeking to get what you can emotionally or physically from him or her. Edification has a very different goal. Edification resists the temptation to satisfy one's own needs and focuses on meeting the needs of the other person instead. It's being more con-cerned about the person you're dating than about yourself.

After Carol and I had been dating for a few years we discovered our timetables weren't the same. I wanted to get married much later in life than Carol did. Based on

that we determined that perhaps God had another plan. So
we broke up. We decided we would not get back together
unless it was with marriage in view.

After we broke up, Carol began to pray that God
would let me date the most gorgeous, talented, and spiritual
person I could hope to meet. Carol wanted to have
confidence that I would not marry her unless I could be
happy with no one else but her. Well, I did meet such a
person. And this woman was unique. Attractive. Smart.
Spiritual. What more could a guy ask? We started dating,
and our relationship leaned heavily on edification. It was
great. But I knew we had no future together. Eventually,
I confessed to her that I knew I was meant to be with
Carol but that our dating had been very beneficial to me.
I grew personally because of her and was encouraged
during our time together. That's the way it ought to work
in dating. Dating other people should prepare you for
God's best, not deplete or damage you emotionally. In fact,

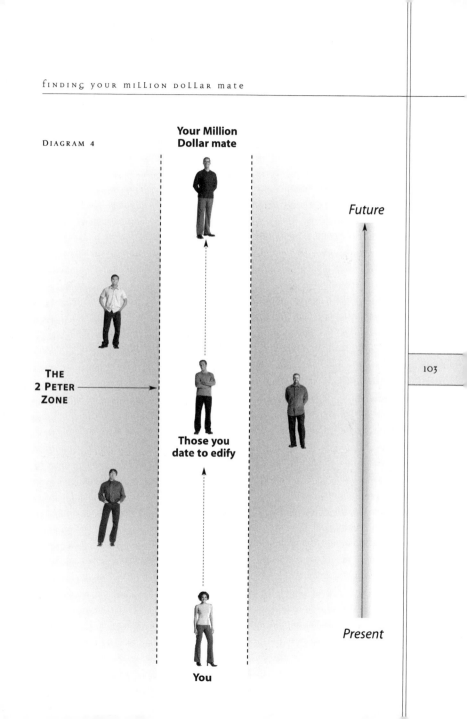

DIAGRAM 4

Your Million Dollar mate

Future

THE 2 PETER ZONE

Those you date to edify

You

Present

I remember telling this girl that my future wife would someday thank her for all she had done for me. A good edifying relationship will benefit you. It won't drain your heart of love and passion but will add strength and character to your soul. That's the difference.

PRINCIPLE #4: PRAY DAILY FOR YOUR FUTURE SPOUSE.

I began praying for my future wife those many years ago even before I understood the meaning of genuine love. You remember the prayer I prayed before I had met Carol, before I knew her name. By praying for your future mate you begin to forge a discipline that will serve you and your marriage for a lifetime.

PRINCIPLE #5: FIND SOME RESPECTED COUNSELORS TO VALIDATE YOUR CHOICE OF A MARRIAGE PARTNER.

Don't go it alone. Find respected counselors, preferably ones more spiritually mature than you and older, to whom you can go for guidance. We each need friends or loved ones who feel free to tell us the truth about ourselves. Seek out those individuals who will tell it like it is. That's especially needed when you're considering marriage. Passionate feeling often blinds us from reality. We need an objective, loving perspective when making such a critical life decision. If possible, start with your parents. If you're older and considering getting married or married again following a divorce or the death of a mate, you might choose a minister, a close friend, or one of your adult children. The point is to resist trying to go it alone. I often tell parents how important it is to make themselves available when the time comes for their children to choose a mate. Here's what worked for me.

When my four kids were young, so little they'd say "yes" to anything, I would lie in bed with them for a few minutes each night. I asked them to agree to let me help them make the decision when eventually they would choose a mate. "Sure, Dad, whatever you say" was their usual reply. And they never gave it another thought. As the years went on I reminded each one of our agreement. Each time they rolled their little eyes and re-upped their commitment.

You can guess what happened. Two of my children are now married. When the time came for them to choose a marriage partner they came to Carol and me for counsel. They remembered that commitment they had made when they were younger. What a privilege it was for us to give our blessing to their choices.

If you're about to choose a mate or agree to a proposal for marriage, avoid making a commitment until someone who loves you and has your best interest at heart has given you feedback. I guarantee you'll never regret it.

Looking back

Before moving to the last chapter you may want to review the five principles I've discussed here. As you do, try to recall how you reacted to each one. Most people never take the time to approach dating, let alone the quest for a mate, with such care and purpose. I recommend that you do so in order to ensure a wise and consistent decision. I'm not trying to take the magic or the romance out of the process. That's all in the mix as far as I'm concerned. You don't want to make such a critical decision based on a scientific formula. But you do want to approach it with wisdom and understanding and with a healthy balance between emotion and discernment. That's what I hope these principles will do for you.

think about it

How are you feeling right now?

Do you feel the dating relationship you're in right now is headed in the right direction?

If not, are you ready to break it off? Do you have someone you trust to help you make that decision?

The last chapter shares the final principle, which is best explained in a story—a personal story from my life that helps to drive the point home.

a PERSONAL
story

PRINCIPLE #6: SET A STANDARD HIGH ENOUGH TO PROTECT YOUR FUTURE.

I was in college, maturing as an individual and growing deeper in my commitment to spiritual things. I had not yet met Carol, and I was going back to college as a sophomore. My friends and I arrived on campus a few days early to get settled in. My best friend and I decided to go to one of the women's dormitories to see many of our friends who would be living there that year.

As soon as we stepped foot in the lobby of the dorm I saw absolutely the most gorgeous girl I think I had ever seen. I pointed her out to my friend, who stood next to me in the lobby. She was stunning. And this was not just my opinion. She won nearly every beauty contest on campus over the next four years. Of course, I was still focused on the physical. Old habits die hard, I guess! Jokingly, I said to my buddy, "You know, if two conditions were met, I'd say that's my million dollar mate." He laughed and asked what I was talking about. I told him the first condition would be that she would have to know me. The second would be that she would have to be a Christian.

He laughed and started to walk away. Before he could take a step the girl turned around and made eye contact with me. I couldn't believe it. She started to come toward me, and as she got closer she said, "Randy, is that you?"

I looked at my friend and said, "There's number one!" My friend couldn't believe his ears.

Puzzled that I didn't recognize her, she said, "Do you not remember me?" I thought, *How could I forget?* She said, "Randy, I was involved with a campus ministry in high school, and we worked together on a beach project one spring break."

I turned to my buddy once again, and smiling like Tom Cruise declared, "There's number two!"

We talked briefly, and she eventually left. My heart pounded as I attempted to make sense of what had just happened. Had I perhaps met my million dollar mate? Maybe all those prayers really did work! It was all too good to be true.

A couple of days later a friend of mine who knew this girl told me she would be interested in going out on a date with me. In time, I worked up the nerve to call her. We talked for over an hour about our past and dreams for the future. At the end of the call we agreed to go together to our next college football game. I was walking on cloud nine!

We had a great time at the game. She seemed so easy to be with and everything looked like a go! We made plans to go out the following evening.

I'll never forget what happened next. Sunday morning after the game I was preparing to go to church. As I stood waiting for my ride an incredible guilt came over me like a dark cloud. Despite my attempts to focus on spiritual things my mind kept going to this girl. It was as if God said to me, "Randy, this is My day and you are more enamored with this girl than you are with Me, your God." She could have been the devil in disguise and I would not have noticed because my emotions had blinded me.

That's when I knew I needed a protective standard.

At that moment I made a vow to the Lord that I would never go out with any girl if I could not pray freely with her on a date. That didn't seem a risk with this particular girl, especially given her religious history. By the way, I don't mean to suggest if someone is not comfortable praying on a date that the person is not spiritual. But for me personally, this represented a standard I knew I needed to set. And it seemed high enough to protect me. Your standard may be different—it may take another shape. Regardless of what it is, I believe you need to set a standard high enough to protect yourself from unhealthy relationships.

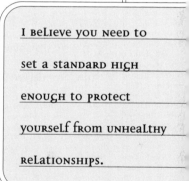

I believe you need to set a standard high enough to protect yourself from unhealthy relationships.

That night after a campus meeting I walked her home, and we talked about a mutual friend who was struggling spiritually. The entire time I kept thinking about the commitment I had made to the Lord that morning. I knew I needed to put this newfound relationship to the test. We stopped by a large tree, and I turned to her and asked, "Why don't we pray together for this guy? I think he needs our prayers." The moment I said that, it was like I had shoved twenty golf balls down her throat all at once. She said, "I'll pray. Trust me, I'll pray, but I just can't pray with you now, like this. That makes me uncomfortable." My heart sank. I knew that what I had heard represented a violation of my standard. I'm not saying that it indicated she wasn't right with God. Yet I knew it wouldn't be right for me to continue dating her. I wanted to shake her and scream, "No! You've got to pray with me!" Instead I walked her home, ending our final date.

Beyond emotions

As I mentioned, her looks took her far in college, and she won awards each year for her striking beauty. Unfortunately, however, the rumor mill suggested that her moral reputation left much to be desired. It turned out she wasn't as spiritually motivated as I had thought, and her life throughout college was spent apart from a close walk with God. I can't help but wonder what would have happened if I had followed my natural desires.

Had it not been for my personal standard, set high enough to matter, who knows where I would be today? Emotions alone can't be trusted. They're a fatal attraction. And the answer to finding the million dollar mate is getting away from the fatal attraction and making the spiritual attraction your ultimate priority. That's a winning game plan.

Let me ask you a question. Where are you in your life right now? Do you believe you're on the right path? Are you walking with God and growing more and more like Him each day? Do you have your priorities straight? Those are critical questions to answer as you continue your quest for your million dollar mate. Ultimately, God cares deeply about you. He knows what you need, and He knows you better than you know yourself. That's why I'm convinced you can trust Him with the deepest longings of your heart.

It's very possible that many people who pick up and read this book are still hurting from a painful past relationship. I know the depth of emotional wounds. I have a few scars myself. And as a pastor I've seen just about everything. But I want you to know that wherever you are in the process, you are not alone. There is One who loves you, Who designed you, and Who calls you by name. And He *does* have a plan. I can't tell you that His plan includes a wonderful marriage. But I can tell you His plan is far better than anything you or I could design.

my pRayeR foR you

Father, I pray for the individual who is holding this book right now. I ask You to provide him or her with the wisdom needed to make a decision about a mate that honors You. And Lord, if Your plan does not include marriage, please grant the grace required to embrace Your wonderful plan. Bless this person with patience and faith to face any uncertain days ahead. Provide courage to make difficult decisions. And give the peace and strength needed to end a relationship headed down the wrong path. Lord, You are good and Your ways are perfect. Together we praise You for loving us enough to set standards for us. Help us to honor them and in doing so to honor You. Thank You, Lord, for the opportunity to share these things with this reader. Bless this reader today, I pray. In Jesus' name, Amen.

NOTES
1. Gloria Goodale, "Singles Weigh in on 'Millionaire,' 'Bachelorette,'" in *The Christian Science Monitor*, 10 January 2003.
http://www.csmonitor.com/2003/0110/p01s01-ussc.html
2. Sources: U.S. Census Bureau, National Center for Health Statistics, Americans for Divorce Reform, Centers for Disease Control and Prevention, Institute for Equality in Marriage, American Association of Single People, Ameristat, Public Agenda. See also on the Web,
http://courses.nnu.edu/ed594gw/U.S.%20Divorce%20Stats.htm
3. 2 Peter 1:3-8, italics added.
4. 2 Peter 1:8, italics added.

"TO THOSE WHO THROUGH the righteousness of our God and Savior Jesus Christ have received a faith as precious as ours: Grace and peace be yours in abundance through the knowledge of God and of Jesus our Lord. His divine power has given us everything we need for life and godliness through our knowledge of him who called us by his own glory and goodness. Through these he has given us his very great and precious promises, so that through them you may participate in the divine nature and escape the corruption in the world caused by evil desires. For this very reason, make every effort to add to your faith goodness; and to goodness, knowledge; and to knowledge, self-control; and to self-control, perseverance; and to perseverance, godliness; and to godliness, brotherly kindness; and to brotherly kindness, love. For if you possess these qualities in increasing measure, they will keep you from being ineffective and unproductive in your knowledge of our Lord Jesus Christ. But if anyone does not have them, he is nearsighted and blind, and has forgotten that he has been cleansed from his past sins. Therefore, my brothers, be all the more eager to make your calling and election sure. For if you do these things, you will never fall, and you will receive a rich welcome into the eternal kingdom of our Lord and Savior Jesus Christ."

(2 Peter 1:2-11 NIV)

NORTHFIELD
PUBLISHING

We hope you enjoyed this product from
Northfield Publishing. Our goal at Northfield is to
provide high-quality, thought-provoking, and practical
books and products that connect truth to the real
needs and challenges of people like you living in our
rapidly changing world. For more information on
other books and products written and produced
from a biblical perspective write to:

Northfield Publishing
215 West Locust Street
Chicago, IL 60610

Finding Your Million Dollar Mate Team

ACQUIRING EDITOR
William L. Thrasher, Jr.

SUBSTANTIVE EDITOR
Mark Tobey

DEVELOPMENTAL EDITOR
Elizabeth Newenhuyse

COPY EDITOR
Cheryl Dunlop

COVER DESIGN
Smartt Guys

INTERIOR DESIGN & ILLUSTRATION
Smartt Guys

PRINTING & BINDING
Lake Book Manufacturing Inc.

The typeface for the text of this book is Belén